FUN MOVERS

Written, designed and illustrated by
Michael Grater

Macdonald

Hanging

Making things is fun, but making fun movers is even better!

Start with a piece of card, a carton or a cylinder. Felt-tips and white PVA glue will soon turn it into something new.

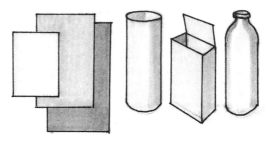

You can add eyes, a nose or a beak to your model, and string or wool for hair. You could decorate the model with paper or cloth and stand it up as a sculpture.

Now tie some thread through a hole at the top of the model. When you hang it up it will move. Sometimes you'll see its front, sometimes its back or sides. Now you have made a simple mobile.

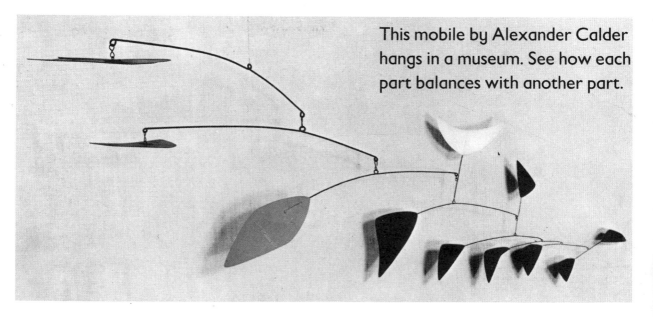

This mobile by Alexander Calder hangs in a museum. See how each part balances with another part.

If you can hang one shape or model so that it moves,
you can hang several together.

You could hang them up and down in a
vertical group or spread them across in
a horizontal group.

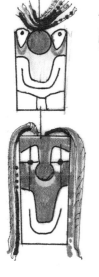

A vertical group is easy. Start with the
bottom shape and work upwards so the
top thread goes on last. You can tape
the thread to the shapes but a mobile
will move better if you tie the thread
through holes.

You will need some canes or sticks for a horizontal
group. Start at the bottom again. When you've hung a
shape at each end of a stick you must find the point
where the stick balances. This is where you tie the next
string.

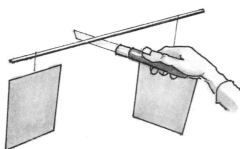

Shapes and

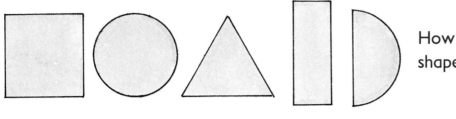

How many different shapes can you think of?

Your mobiles can be just shapes, but what colours can you add to make them look better?

How many different patterns could you draw on the shapes?

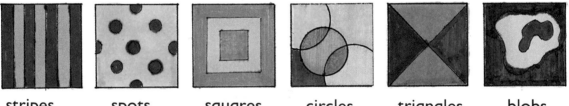

stripes   spots   squares   circles   triangles   blobs

There are endless different shapes, colours and patterns.

As you make more fun movers you'll find you get better at thinking of new shapes and patterns. Look around you for ideas – you are surrounded by different patterns.

What sort of models could you hang as mobiles?

How about people?

. . . or fish?

. . . or flowers?

. . . or flying things?

Try making a list of different things you could hang as mobiles. Think of things that float in water or fly in the air. You'll be surprised how long your list is!

Forms and

A flat shape has only two dimensions (2-D) – it has width and height but no depth. If you give it depth by folding it, it becomes three-dimensional (3-D) and has form. Try cutting the same shape out several times and see how many different folded forms you can make.

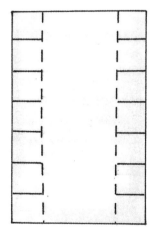

You can cut into the edge of a shape and fold it. Try cutting out a card rectangle. Mark it up as shown, dividing it into three parts. Cut on the thick lines and score and fold on the dotted ones.

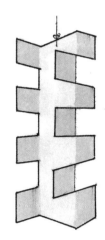

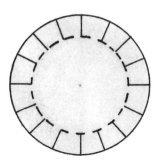

Try doing the same with other shapes or the 3-D forms made from rectangles.

You can turn any shape into an interesting form but it is likely to work better if you use a ruler to mark straight edges. Use a scissor point to score folds.

Keep your eyes open for things people throw away,
you'll soon find lots of new ideas for models and forms.

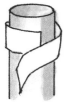

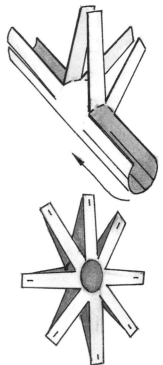

A kitchen roll card cylinder is very
useful. You can measure round it with a
strip of paper. Open out the strip and
measure or fold it into equal parts.
Transfer these marks to the cylinder
and use a ruler to mark it out as shown.
Cut the strips and fold them back and
staple them together. Try fixing two of
the forms together.

The mobiles below were made from paper cups and
plates, and the spiral mobile was made with spring
clothes pegs arranged on 5 mm wooden dowel.

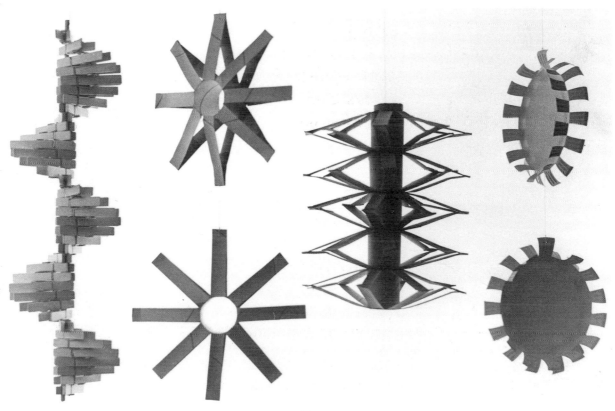

FUN MOVERS from Nature

Fishes, birds, insects, flowers, leaves, seeds, waves, clouds, or anything else you can think of could be an idea for a fun mover from the natural world. Use pictures in books or, better still, look at the real thing.

For example, this picture of a fish will start you off. If the real thing is very complicated and you need to simplify it, try looking at it with your eyes half-shut.

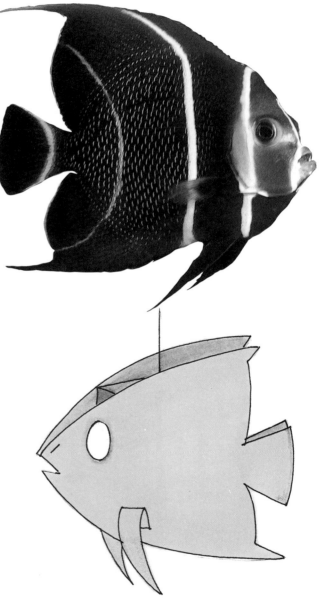

A picture will help with your model's shape and decoration. Decorate both sides of the model.

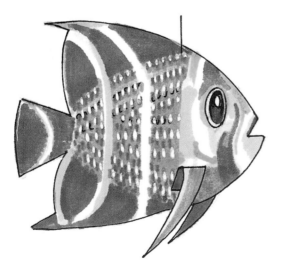

You can give a model a third dimension by fixing two shapes the same size on each side of a spacer or small box.

Try making birds from card cylinders. Pictures will help you with shapes of beaks and heads. What differences can you see in the birds' feet?

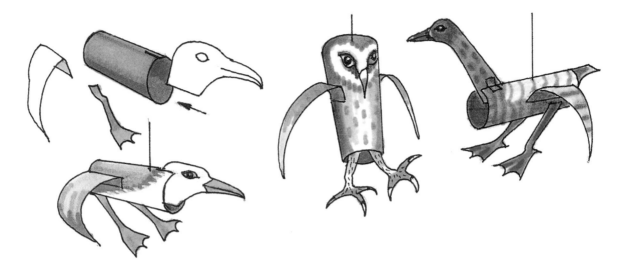

Butterflies are easy to model and very colourful! Another insect you might try is a moth. Do you know the differences between a moth and a butterfly?

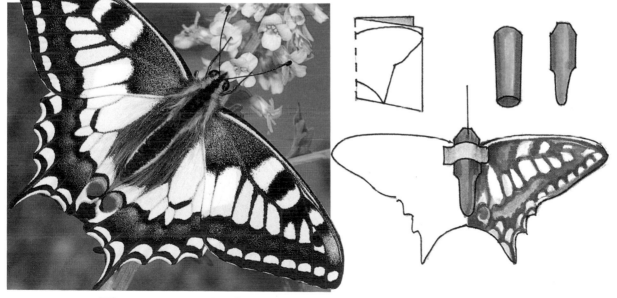

The more you look at nature and use what you see to help you make models, the better your fun movers will be. Why not brighten up your bedroom or classroom with some of your mobiles?

FUN MOVERS from the human world

Library books will show you how people learned to fly in the air and out into Space. You've seen films about flying and Space travel, so why not design and make your own flying machines?

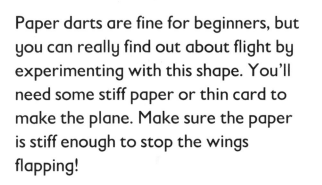

Paper darts are fine for beginners, but you can really find out about flight by experimenting with this shape. You'll need some stiff paper or thin card to make the plane. Make sure the paper is stiff enough to stop the wings flapping!

Carefully trace out one side of the plane shape. Take your paper or card and fold it neatly down the centre. Transfer the tracing so that the centre line runs along the fold. Cut out the shape along the solid lines. Gently score and fold the dotted lines.

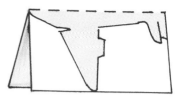

Fix a paper clip to the front of the plane and tape the wings together at the top. Now your plane is ready to fly. You may need to adjust the angles on the wing folds.

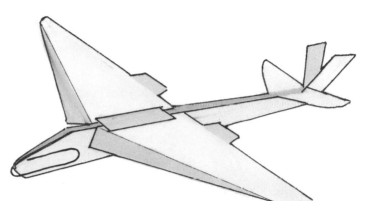

Experiment with different planes. Your flight trials will show you a lot about how planes fly. A book about flight will help you understand how your models fly and how you can make more experiments.

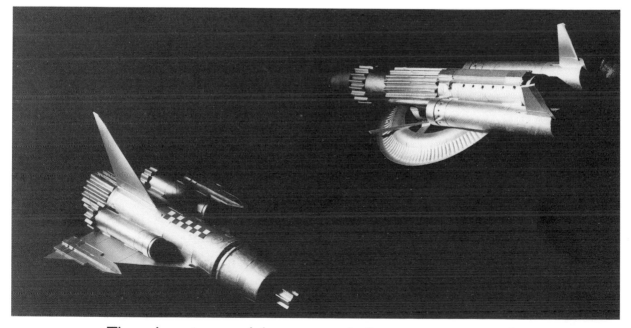

These hanging models were made from scrap materials. Aluminium spray paint made them even more realistic.

Twister

Why do you think some of your hanging fun movers move better than others? Try this simple experiment.

Cut four pieces of card 10 × 15 cm and make a hole in the centre of one of the short sides. Tie some thread through the hole and run with one of the cards trailing behind you. What happens?

Score the next piece of card from the top corners to the centre point on the opposite side. Fold the triangles in opposite ways. What happens if you run with it now? You may need to swing it about a bit, but it should spin – the air current is being funnelled along the folded edges, making the card rotate like a propeller. Try some other card spinners.

How does the spinner work if you thread it at the other end?

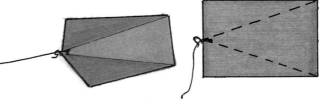

How does it work if you fold it a different way?

Try all four spinners and you'll see how the air can be used to make a regular spinning movement.

You can use your discoveries to make some fun twisters.

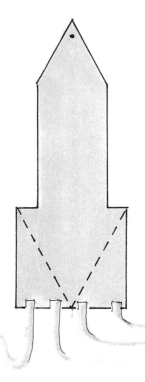

Measure and mark out a twister rocket with fin shapes at its base.

Decorate the rocket on both sides and bend over the fins. Tape some kitchen foil strips to the fins. They will trail like smoke if you run with the rocket.

What else could you make into a twister – a twisting witch? Whatever you make, keep it symmetrical, that is if you fold it down the middle both sides are the same.

You can hang twisters outside on a clothes line or a tree. If you use thin, strong thread your twisters will move in the wind, especially on a blustery day!

Wind shape Fun Movers

After twisters you can try other forms that work in air currents.

Twist a strip of paper or thin card 2.5 × 60 cm into a figure 8. Fix the ends of the strip together with staples or glue. The loops should be the same size. You may need to try this a few times to get it right.

At the cross-over point in the centre make a half cut on each strip so that they can be locked together.

When you have made the figure 8, fix a thread at the top and try running with it. If you've made it well it will spin. You could hang up brightly coloured wind shapes indoors and outside, and shapes made of foil-covered card will look especially attractive.

Propeller and windmill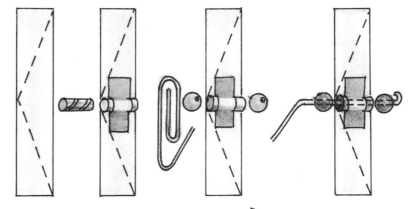

Another wind form you can try is a propeller. Cut a piece of card 3 × 15 cm. Score and fold from the corners to the centre opposite. Tape a piece of drinking straw across the centre. Find a paper clip and two small round beads and straighten the clip to fix as shown. Now tape the propeller to a simple card plane and see what happens when you run with it.

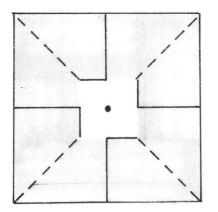

To make a windmill, cut a 10 cm square of card and mark it as shown, with a 3 cm square at the centre. Cut on the heavy lines and score the dotted lines. Fold the sails and mount them on a straightened paper clip, using beads and a straw spacer.

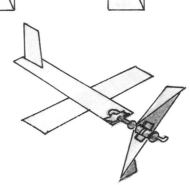

You can fix the sails to a plastic bottle filled with water and experiment to see where it catches the wind best. A hair-drier is useful for this.

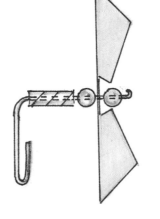

17

Rocker

So far, you have made forms that go round and round — they rotate. But there are other sorts of movement that can be used for fun movers.

A wheel rotates on its axle. But if you cut the wheel in half it would have to move in a different way — it would rock.

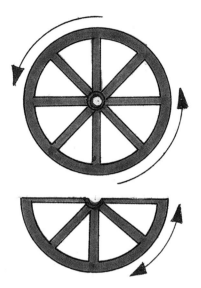

Use a pair of compasses to draw a circle about 15 cm across on some card. Carefully cut it out and fold it in half. Now you have a simple rocking form which you can turn into all sorts of fun movers.

You can add figures to the rocker, and when you have made a working rocker you could add other moving bits. Try a moustache loosely fixed with a push-through metal paper fastener. It will move as your rocker moves.

A paper plate scored in half with a scissor point and folded can be the starting point for a rocker.

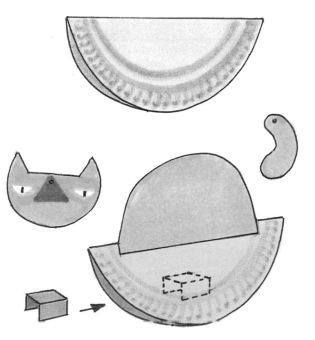

If the rocker tends to slide open, tape a card bracket on the inside.

Friendly card

You can cut specially-shaped, folded rockers that you could send as cards to friends or relatives.

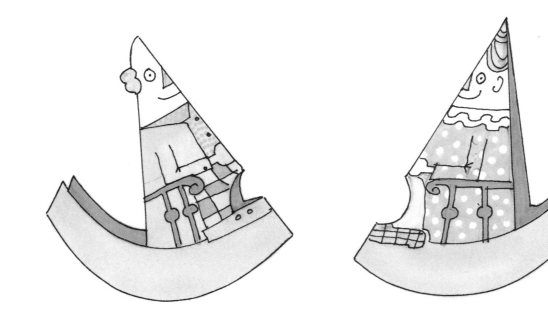

Before you decorate the card you should cut out the rocking shape to make sure it rocks well. The shape on this page will get you started. Cut it from a piece of card folded double on the dotted line.

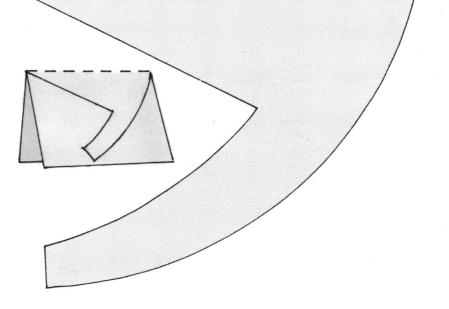

Rocking toy FUN MOVERS

Now you are ready to make some more complicated rocking toys.

Find the centre of a paper plate by measuring across the diameter. Measure out from this line to draw two parallel lines. Score them and fold the sides down to make a rocker with a platform. Fix a card bracket on the inside to hold the sides in place.

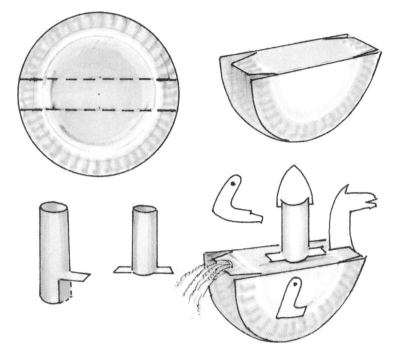

Tape some toy people to the rocker top. If you make the toys carefully they will be strong enough to give away as presents.

Cylinder swinger

If you hang up a model it can rotate or swing like a pendulum. But your model will move even better if it is flexible and has its own movement as well.

Think of all the cylindrical forms we throw away every day – card rolls and containers, plastic bottles, drink cans, bits of plastic pipe lagging, and so on.

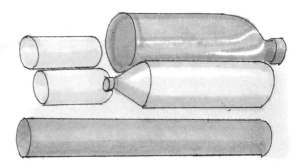

Now think of the cylinders in a different way.

If you tie two cylinders together, just tight enough for them to move, you can roll them round each other.

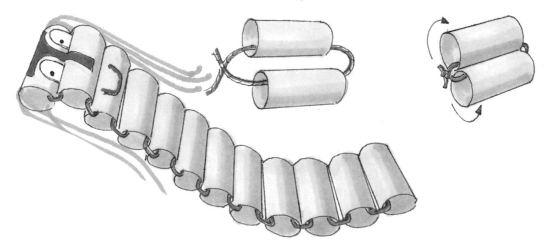

If you join lots of the cylinders you have collected you can make wonderfully flexible forms. Now you can use them to make fun movers.

Plastic bottle beasts are very rare but there are millions of empty plastic bottles. Plastic bottles hang well because they are light, and when they are put together they will swing easily in the wind outside.

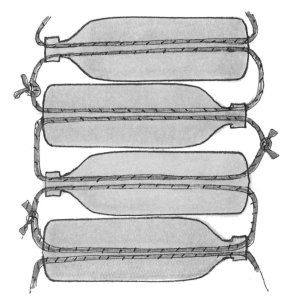

To string plastic bottles together you must first make holes in their bases. Use a bradawl or a sharp, pointed instrument for this. Be very careful when you use a bradawl - wear a thick, protective glove on the hand holding the bottle.

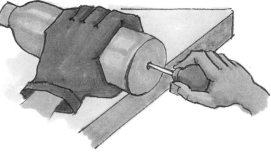

Bouncer

Corrugated paper is very flexible and you can use it to make bouncers which you can hang on elastic.

Cut out some corrugated people shapes as large as you can. You'll get very strange effects if you bounce them on the elastic. Try making them dance to your favourite music. You could even work out a ballet for your bouncers.

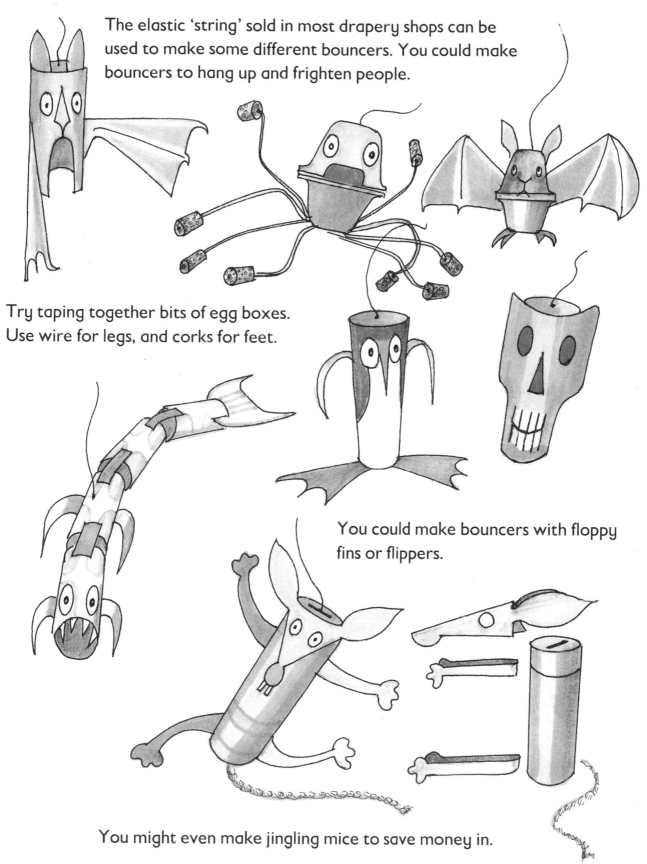

The elastic 'string' sold in most drapery shops can be used to make some different bouncers. You could make bouncers to hang up and frighten people.

Try taping together bits of egg boxes. Use wire for legs, and corks for feet.

You could make bouncers with floppy fins or flippers.

You might even make jingling mice to save money in.

Springback Fun Movers

Plastic bottles that contain fizzy drinks have round bottoms. They only stand up because they are fixed into flat plastic cups. But you can have lots of fun with these bottles if you take the cups off.

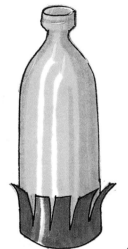

Remove the cup by cutting down from its top and prising it away from the bottle. The cup is fixed with spots of glue but any that's left can be cleaned off with white spirit.

Put a weight in the bottom of the bottle. Ball bearings are best but small nails or washers will do if you can't get ball bearings.

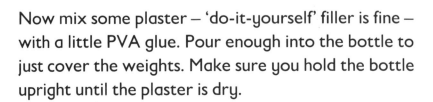

Now mix some plaster – 'do-it-yourself' filler is fine – with a little PVA glue. Pour enough into the bottle to just cover the weights. Make sure you hold the bottle upright until the plaster is dry.

When the plaster is dry the bottle should stand up by itself. If the weight in the bottom is right your springback will always jump back when you try to push it over.

When your springback works properly you can decorate it with paper cut-outs stuck down with tape, and wool tied to the neck. Now you have made a modern version of a very old-fashioned toy that has amused children for many years.

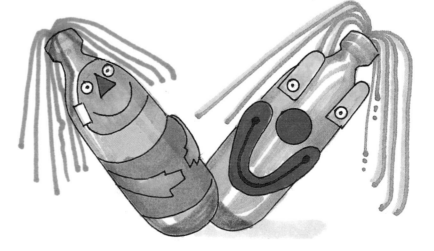

Flicker

When you make things, you'll see how they move in air currents or how gravity makes them fall. But you can find other things to add even more movement to your models. Try metal paper fasteners.

Join two lolly sticks (or bits of plastic or stiff card) together with a paper fastener. You have made a simple lever – a quick flick of one stick moves the other.

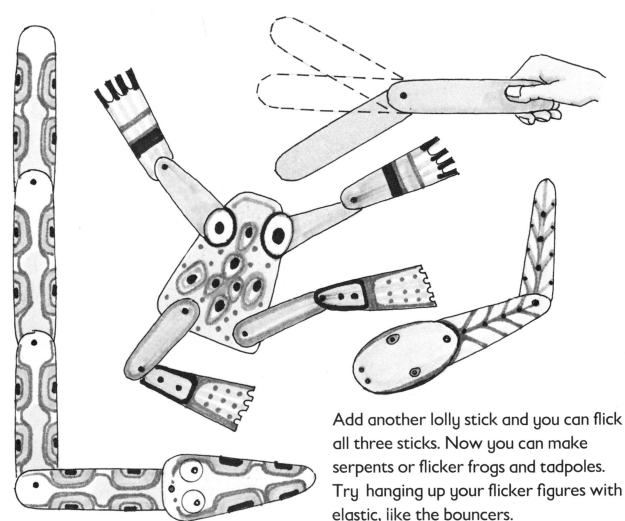

Add another lolly stick and you can flick all three sticks. Now you can make serpents or flicker frogs and tadpoles. Try hanging up your flicker figures with elastic, like the bouncers.

Stretcher FUN MOVERS

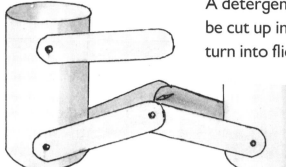

A detergent bottle with its top cut off can be cut up into lots of strips of plastic to turn into flickers and stretchers.

You can use flickers on models to make stretchers, toys that can be moved into all sorts of positions – like the wrestlers with jointed limbs on cylinder bodies.

Why not make a troop of acrobats? What other people or animals might you see together in groups? Try and work out some flickers or stretchers of your own.

Going on with

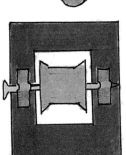

Pull-along toys are always fun. The problem is making their wheels. Try using a nail for an axle and a cotton-reel for a wheel.

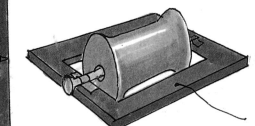

If you firmly tape the nail with its wheel to a stiff card you will have a chassis for whatever sort of toy you want to make. An empty container fixed to the chassis can be decorated to make your toy.

There are many more ways to make fun movers. Look at the containers that you have collected and think of all the different ideas you've already tried – what other things can you make that will move in some way?